CONTENTS

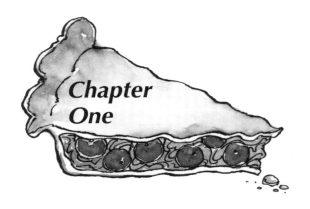

Chapter One

Tommy Taylor loved pie. He loved every kind of pie in the world. Every morning, when Tommy woke up, he would sing:

"Pie, pie, beautiful pie,
Lemon, cherry, sweet blackberry,
What would I do without pie?"

Tommy loved pie so much that he wouldn't eat anything else. His parents had a huge bookcase full of cookbooks. All of the recipes were for pie.

There were breakfast recipes for oatmeal pie, granola pie, toast pie, and, of course, bacon-and-egg pie. There were pie recipes for lunch, dinner, and dessert.

Tommy's parents spent hours searching through the books for new pie recipes that would tantalize their son's taste buds.

Whenever Tommy's teacher asked the class to write stories, Tommy always wrote about fantastic pies, such as cranberry-and-custard pie topped with chewy caramel, or mango-and-marshmallow pie sprinkled with nuts.

As soon as Tommy finished a story, he'd sing:

"Pie, pie, beautiful pie,
Lemon, cherry, sweet blackberry,
What would I do without pie?"

Tommy's class thought he was a little strange. But he knew they wouldn't think so when he grew up to be a pie maker *extraordinaire*!

7

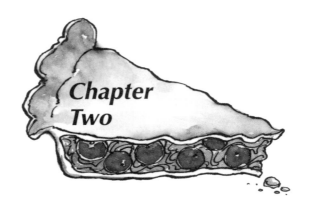

Chapter Two

One morning, as Tommy sat at the breakfast table eating his cornflakes-and-peaches pie, he heard a huge rumbling, grumbling sound.

The floor shook, the dishes slid off the shelves, and the clock fell off the wall. Tommy only just managed to rescue his pie before his mom pulled him under the table. She thought it was an earthquake.

9

When Tommy's parents were sure that the shaking had stopped, they all ventured outside to see what had caused the commotion. There, at the bottom of the Taylors' steps, was the largest mountain of mud they had ever seen.

The mud mountain spread out past their front yard, across the sidewalk and road, right over to the playground of Tommy's school. Tommy and his parents stared at the mud in amazement.

The mud mountain was so tall that Mr. Taylor had to climb onto the roof of their house just to see over it. From up there, he saw the mayor of the town, with a loudspeaker in his hand, standing on top of a fire-truck platform.

"Hear me, good citizens of Smallbrook," the mayor shouted through his loudspeaker. "We have a rather big problem. A mountain of a problem, you might say," he joked, although it was no joking matter.

"This pile of mud that has slid into our town must be moved," the mayor continued. "It's blocking the road, and our children won't be able to get to school."

The mayor looked quite serious. "It's very important that we get rid of this mud in the next twenty-four hours, before the national town inspector makes her annual visit. We never win anything in the Best Town contest, but we don't want Smallbrook to lose its reputation as a beautiful little town."

17

The mayor raised his arms in the air. "I'm asking all the people in Smallbrook to put on their thinking caps and come up with a way to clean up this muddy mess. This afternoon, the town's homing pigeon will fly over the mud mountain and visit every house in town."

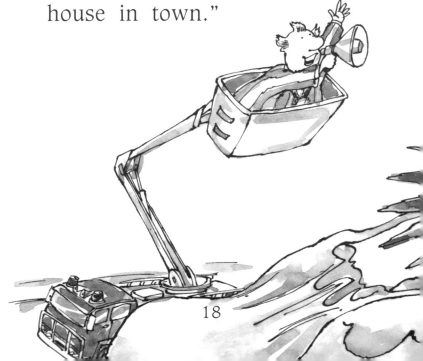

The mayor continued his speech, waving his hands, "Please write down any ideas about how we can move the mud and put them into the homing pigeon's mailbag. I'm sure that if we all try hard, we can come up with a solution to our problem."

19

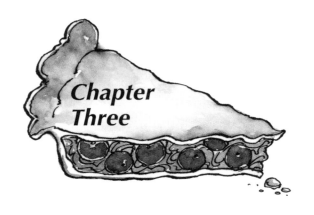

Chapter Three

So the Taylors set about thinking of a solution to Smallbrook's muddy dilemma. They called a family meeting and sat around the table, brainstorming ideas. Mr. Taylor thought that if everyone in town pitched in with their shovels and wheelbarrows, they could move the mud away.

Mrs. Taylor said, "What a wonderful opportunity this is.

The people of Smallbrook can all work together."

But Tommy pointed out that there was nowhere to move the mud to in Smallbrook.

21

Then Mrs. Taylor suggested that everyone in Smallbrook could donate a few plants from their gardens and turn the mud mountain into one huge hillside flower garden.

Mr. Taylor said, "Fantastic, that will make Smallbrook look very beautiful indeed."

But Tommy reminded his parents that, although it would be a beautiful sight, the road would still be blocked, and the children would be unable to get to school.

Finally, it was Tommy's turn to come up with an idea. He sat at the table, scratching his head, but nothing sprang to mind. Tommy decided that perhaps he needed a little snack to help him along.

As he strolled over to the cupboard, Tommy sang:

"Pie, pie, beautiful pie,
Lemon, cherry, sweet blackberry,
What would I do without pie?"

Suddenly, an idea hit him like a custard pie in the face. "Of course! We could turn the ugly mud mountain into a beautiful mud pie. The messiest, murkiest, muckiest, dirtiest mud pie in the whole world!" exclaimed Tommy.

Following a wonderful lunch of fish pie, Mr. Taylor climbed back up onto the roof with Tommy's plan written on a piece of paper. He carefully tucked the plan into the homing pigeon's mailbag. After climbing down again, Mr. Taylor waited with Mrs. Taylor and Tommy for the mayor's next announcement.

29

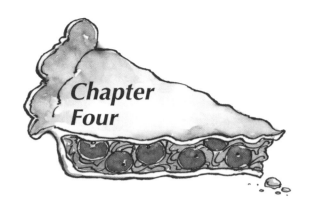

Chapter
Four

Later, the mayor once again addressed the town. "Worthy people of Smallbrook, it's with pleasure that I can tell you that we have found a solution. We've had some clever ideas and some not-so-clever ideas, but the best suggestion has come from Tommy Taylor. Smallbrook's going to become the proud owner of the biggest mud pie in the world!"

Early the next morning, the entire town set to work under Tommy's direction. All of the town's builders and construction workers gathered together. They mixed strong lightweight cement, which the town's potters, plasterers, and sculptors then molded into a gigantic pie dish.

The rest of the townspeople emptied the water from the school swimming pool and then began to fill up the pool with mud. It was hard, messy, dirty work, but they enjoyed themselves. They all laughed and joked as they shoveled the mud from the mountain into the pool.

Under Tommy's watchful eyes, the mud in the pool was mixed with water and other ingredients until it was the messiest, murkiest, muckiest, dirtiest mud possible.

After Tommy had approved each batch of mud, helicopters, carrying huge buckets, were brought in to move the muddy mixture from the pool to the pie dish.

It took all day and all night, but finally the mud mountain disappeared. In its place was the biggest mud pie in the entire world.

Cranes were brought in and the pie was lifted up, slowly but surely, and placed on top of tall pillars, right in the center of Smallbrook. It was an impressive sight.

41

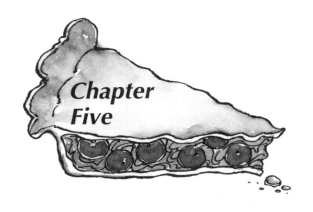

Chapter Five

As the townspeople stood admiring the new monument, the national town inspector pulled up in her limousine. When she stepped out of the car, a hushed silence fell over the people.

The inspector stared at the huge mud pie in amazement. Then she laughed. "Some towns have a giant carrot. Others have a giant strawberry.

But I have never seen a town with a giant mud pie before. Smallbrook wins first prize in the Best Town contest." Then she handed the mayor a huge silver cup.

The mayor smiled proudly, accepted the cup, and then announced, "I think we all know to whom this cup belongs. Tommy Taylor, do you have anything you would like to say?"

"Only this," said Tommy, and he began to sing:

"Mud, mud, beautiful mud,
Messy, murky, mucky, and dirty,
What would I do without mud?"

The people clapped and cheered for Tommy Taylor, mud-pie maker *extraordinaire*!

FROM THE AUTHOR

One of the great things about pie is that it comes in so many different flavors. I had a lot of fun writing this story, thinking of all the different kinds of pie you could have. Perhaps, one day, I'll try mango-and-marshmallow pie sprinkled with nuts. But I think I'll skip oatmeal pie!

Not only is pie good to eat, but it's also fun to make. And the pie that is probably the most fun to create is a messy, murky, mucky, and dirty mud pie.

My daughter, Lucretia, loves to make mud pies. So if a mountain of mud lands in our street, she'll know what to do!

Frances Bacon

FROM THE ILLUSTRATOR

When I illustrate a book, I like to do some research. So, after a day of rain, I took a wheelbarrow out, in search of mud, real sticky mud, the sort that makes a *slop* sound when you walk in it.

At the bottom of a hill, I found some. Since I had forgotten to take a shovel, I scooped the mud into the wheelbarrow with my hands.

Back at my studio, I discovered I had acquired a kind of muddy Midas touch. Pencils, pens, and paper were transformed into globs of mud before my eyes. So if you find a muddy blob on some of the pictures in this book, you'll know why!

Ian Forss

Imagine That!

Fuzz and the Glass Eye
Which Way, Jack?
The Wish Fish
Famous Animals

Pie, Pie, Beautiful Pie
My Word! How Absurd
You Can Canoe!
A World of Imagination

Written by **Frances Bacon**
Illustrated by **Ian Forss**

© 1999 Shortland Publications Inc.

05 04 03 02 01 00
10 9 8 7 6 5 4 3 2

Published in the United States by

a division of Reed Elsevier Inc.
500 Coventry Lane
Crystal Lake, IL 60014

Printed in Hong Kong
ISBN: 0-7901-1833-5